ISAAC ASIMOV'S NEW LIBRARY OF THE UNIVERSE

THE SUN AND ITS SECRETS

BY ISAAC ASIMOV
WITH REVISIONS AND UPDATING BY FRANCIS REDDY

Gareth Stevens Publishing
MILWAUKEE

For a free color catalog describing Gareth Stevens' list of high-quality books, call 1-800-542-2595 (USA) or 1-800-461-9120 (Canada). Gareth Stevens' Fax: (414) 225-0377.

Library of Congress Cataloging-in-Publication Data

Asimov, Isaac.
    The sun and its secrets / by Isaac Asimov and Francis Reddy.
       p. cm. — (Isaac Asimov's New library of the universe)
    Rev. ed. of: The sun. 1988.
    Includes index.
    ISBN 0-8368-1135-6
    1. Sun—Juvenile literature. [1. Sun.] I. Reddy, Francis, 1959-. II. Asimov, Isaac.
    The sun. III. Title. IV. Series: Asimov, Isaac. New library of the universe.
    QB521.5.A84   1994
    523.7—dc20   94-15422

This edition first published in 1994 by
Gareth Stevens Publishing
1555 North RiverCenter Drive, Suite 201
Milwaukee, Wisconsin 53212, USA

Project editor: Barbara J. Behm
Design adaptation: Helene Feider
Production director: Susan Ashley
Editorial assistant: Diane Laska
Picture research: Kathy Keller
Artwork commissioning: Kathy Keller and Laurie Shock

Printed in the United States of America

1 2 3 4 5 6 7 8 9 99 98 97 96 95 94

To bring this classic of young people's information up to date, the editors at Gareth Stevens Publishing have selected two noted science authors, Greg Walz-Chojnacki and Francis Reddy. Walz-Chojnacki and Reddy coauthored the recent book *Celestial Delights: The Best Astronomical Events Through 2001*.

Walz-Chojnacki is also the author of the book *Comet: The Story Behind Halley's Comet* and various articles about the space program. He was an editor of *Odyssey*, an astronomy and space technology magazine for young people, for eleven years.

Reddy is the author of nine books, including *Halley's Comet*, *Children's Atlas of the Universe*, *Children's Atlas of Earth Through Time*, and *Children's Atlas of Native Americans*, plus numerous articles. He was an editor of *Astronomy* magazine for several years.

CONTENTS

We live in an enormously large place – the Universe. It's only in the last fifty-five years or so that we've found out how large it probably is. It's only natural that we would want to understand the place in which we live, so scientists have developed instruments – such as radio telescopes, satellites, probes, and many more – that have told us far more about the Universe than could possibly be imagined.

We have seen planets up close. We have learned about quasars and pulsars, black holes, and supernovas. We have gathered amazing data about how the Universe may have come into being and how it may end. Nothing could be more astonishing.

But of all the portions of the Universe we see in the sky, the most spectacular is the Sun. When it is shining, it drowns out everything else. It is so bright, we cannot look at it directly. In fact, we had better not try because it can quickly damage our eyes. When the Sun shines, all is bright. When clouds cover the Sun, the day is gloomy. At night, when the Sun is not overhead, the sky is dark. All the world depends on the Sun.

Isaac Asimov

Origins of the Sun and Planets

How did the Sun and planets come to be? The origins of the Sun and planets began about five billion years ago in the heart of a swirling cloud of gas and dust. Part of the cloud became compressed and began to contract. This loose ball of gas and dust kept contracting as gravity pulled material toward its center. As the gas ball became more compressed, the temperature of the ball began to increase. Eventually, the temperature deep inside the ball reached millions of degrees. It was so hot that the center of the gas ball began generating its own energy. Our Sun had begun to shine! In addition, large clumps of material circled the newborn Sun. These clumps would become the planets, moons, comets, and asteroids of our Solar System.

Top: The Great Nebula in Orion glows with the light of hot, young stars. Behind the colorful nebula lies the dark, dusty cloud in which new stars are born. Our Sun formed in just such a cloud.

Bottom: Birth of the Sun in a cloud of gas and dust.

1. Billions of years ago, part of the cloud began to contract into a ball of gas.

2. Continuing contraction heated the glowing ball of gas.

3. Deep inside the gas ball, temperatures rose so high that nuclear reactions began to produce energy. The Sun was born!

4. Planets, moons, comets, and asteroids formed as the Sun was created. They continue to orbit the Sun today.

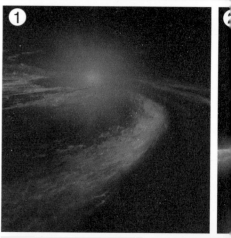

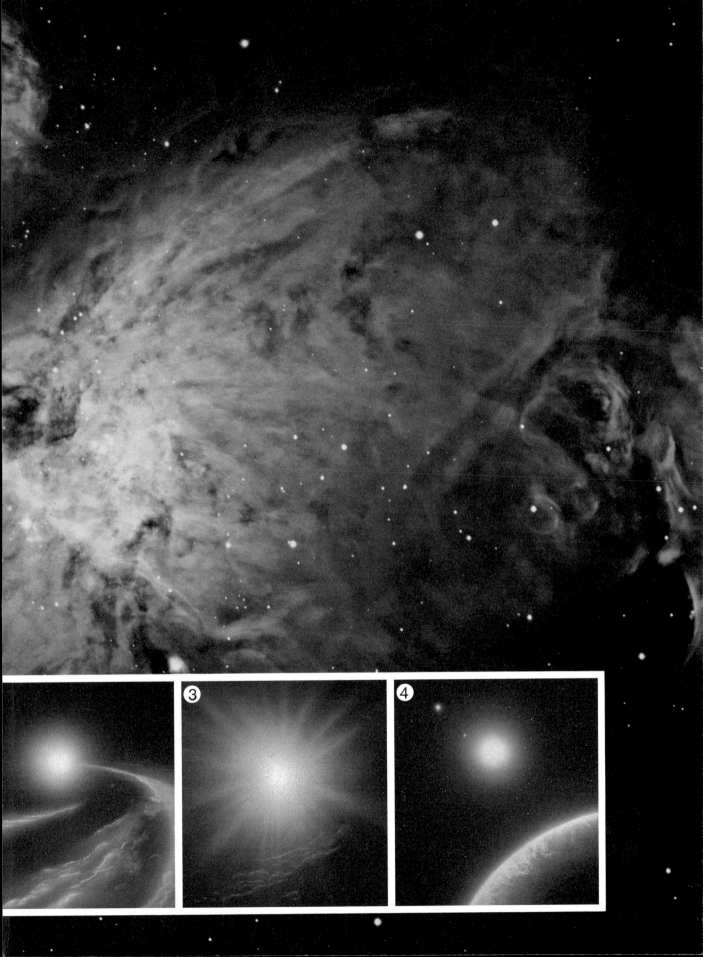

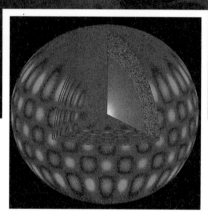

Above: The Sun is a natural hydrogen bomb. Here is a human-made, exploding hydrogen bomb used as a weapon. *Inset:* A computer image shows how the Sun wavers. Red areas move back. Blue areas move forward. Pictures like this help scientists learn about the structure and inside activity of the Sun.

Opposite, above: A neutrino detector allows scientists to trap and count tiny particles from the Sun called neutrinos.

Right: Hydrogen turns into helium in the Sun's fiery heart, generating the energy that reaches us on every sunbeam.

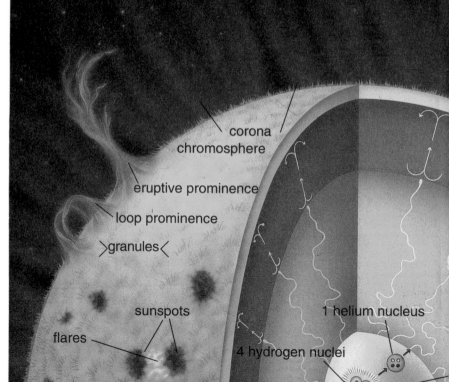

corona

chromosphere

eruptive prominence

loop prominence

>granules<

sunspots

flares

1 helium nucleus

4 hydrogen nuclei

What Makes the Sun Shine?

We know that the Sun has existed for billions of years, but what makes it shine? The Sun's energy comes from nuclear reactions that occur deep inside it. The Sun is about three-quarters hydrogen. Its center is so hot and dense that hydrogen atoms can fuse to form another chemical element — helium. Each second, the Sun transforms about 700 million tons of hydrogen into 695 million tons of helium. What becomes of the missing material? It is changed into the energy that heats and lights our star. One day scientists hope to control these same reactions to produce energy from the hydrogen in seawater here on Earth.

❓ *The case of the missing neutrinos*

When hydrogen fuses to helium deep in the Sun's center, tiny particles called neutrinos are produced. These are hard to detect. But in the 1970s, an American scientist, Raymond Davis, developed a way. He tried to trap at least a few neutrinos that came from the Sun. He didn't expect to trap many. The number he did trap was one-third the number he had expected to get. The experiment has been repeated over and over, and each time there is a neutrino shortage. Why? Do scientists have the wrong idea about what goes on inside the Sun?

solar wind
coronal hole
convection zone
radiation zone
photosphere
core

Our Massive and Powerful Sun

The brilliant star, our Sun, is huge. It is about 93 million miles (150 million kilometers) away from Earth. At that distance, it *must* be huge to be seen as such a large ball. It is about 865,000 miles (1,390,000 km) in diameter, 108 times as wide as Earth. It has 333,400 times the mass of Earth. In fact, it has almost 1,000 times the combined mass of all the planets, satellites, asteroids, and comets circling it! The Sun's gravitational pull is so strong that it holds all those objects in orbit and forces them to move around it. Our Earth is one of those planets turning around the Sun, making one complete circle in a year.

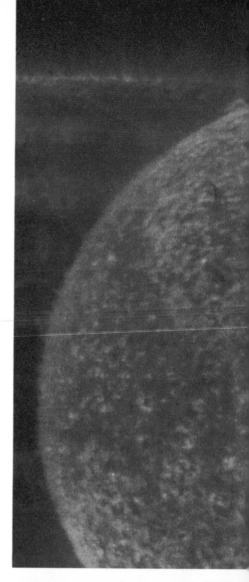

! *Our Earth-Moon system – tiny beside the Sun!*

Here's one way to think about the Sun's size. Imagine that Earth is placed in the center of the Sun. Also imagine that the Moon is circling Earth at its usual distance of 238,820 miles (384,320 km) away. The Moon, as it circled, would still be inside the Sun. In fact, it would be only a little over halfway to the Sun's surface. In other words, the Sun alone is bigger than the entire Earth-Moon system! Astronauts have traveled from Earth to the Moon, but they have not yet gone far enough to match the distance from the Sun's center to the Sun's surface.

Top: The Sun erupting. The size of Earth as shown in this picture gives you an idea of how huge solar eruptions can be. If we could harness the energy from an eruption like this, there would be enough power on Earth for the next two thousand years. This eruption occurred on June 10, 1973, and was recorded by *Skylab 2.*

Bottom: As Earth revolves around, or orbits, the Sun, the northern and southern ends of Earth's axis take turns tilting toward the Sun. Summer comes to the hemisphere that tilts toward the Sun; winter comes to the hemisphere that tilts away from the Sun.

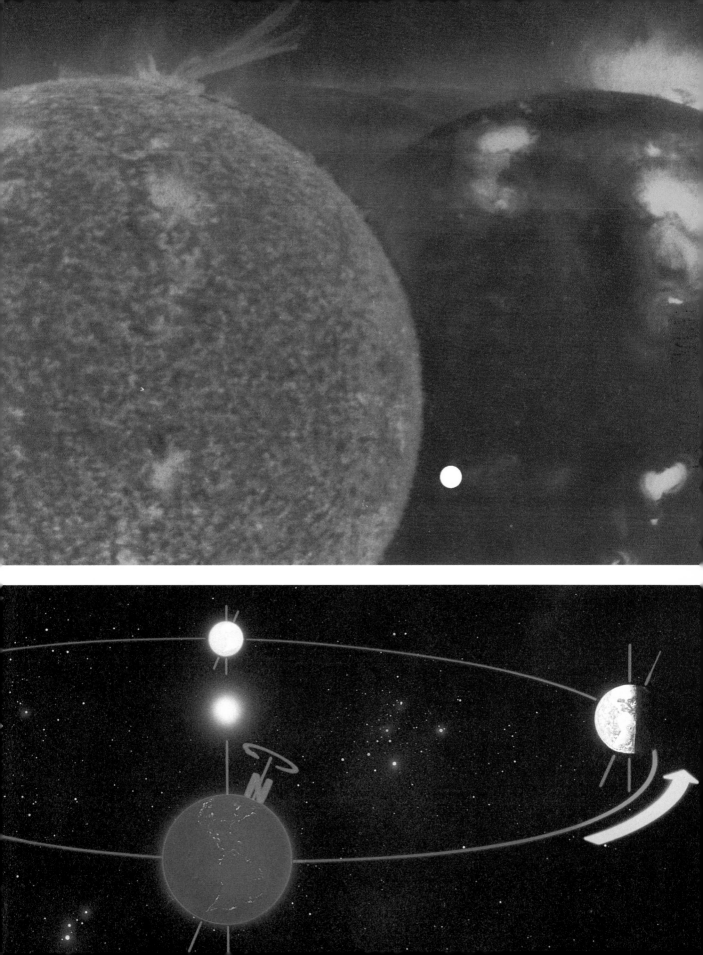

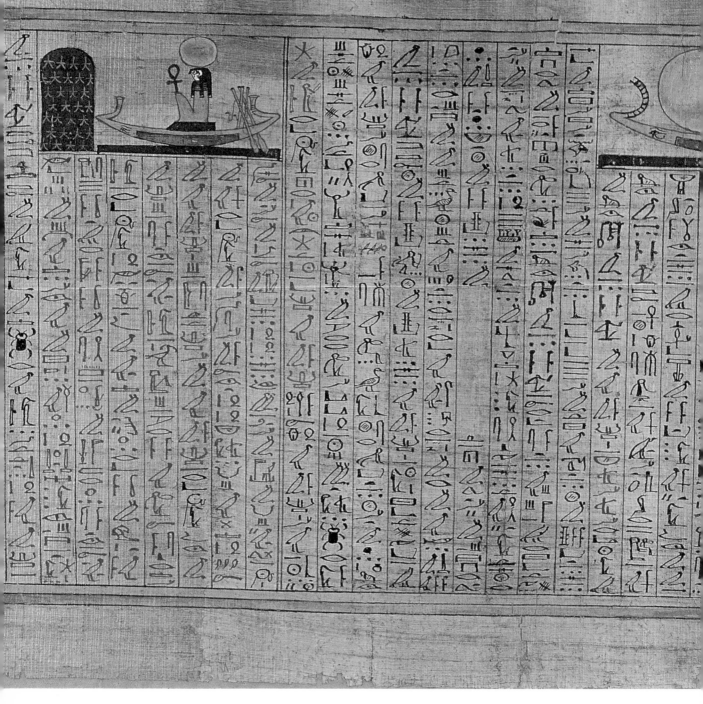

Above: Ra, the Sun god of ancient Egyptian mythology, was usually shown with a hawk's head on a human body. Mythology says that he controlled the Universe by rowing the Sun across the sky in his boat, taking the world from day to night and back to day again. Many ancient religions held that the creation of the world was made possible by the power of the Sun and its gods.

Sun Worship

Why do we need this powerful star? At night in ancient times, our world was dark except for the dim light of a campfire or the Moon. It was also cold, especially in the winter and especially when the campfire burned low. How relieved people were when the Sun finally rose! Then the light came, and Earth was heated again.

When you think about the Sun's light and warmth, it's no wonder many primitive people worshiped it as a god. They had good reason. Without the Sun, everything would freeze, and plants that provide food would not grow. Without the Sun, in fact, there would be no life on Earth.

Our Sun: not too big, not too small – just right!

The more massive a star, the shorter its lifetime. A massive star has more hydrogen in order for it to undergo what is known as fusion to produce energy. But the hydrogen in a massive star must fuse very rapidly to produce the energy to keep the star from collapsing under its own gravitational pull. An extremely massive star might survive only 100 million years.

Then it would explode and collapse. That's not enough time for life to develop. A very small star, on the other hand, might last 200 billion years. But a small star wouldn't produce enough energy for life to develop. Our middle-sized star, the Sun, is just right. It not only produces enough energy for life but also will survive for a total of 10 billion years.

11

In Constant Motion

The Sun's surface is not even. Parts of it are always rising, and other parts are sinking. It's a little bit like the water of Earth's oceans that rises and falls in waves. As a result of this rising and falling, the surface of the Sun seems to consist of granules of matter packed closely together. A granule of the Sun looks small to us from Earth; but on the average, each one is about 600 miles (1,000 km) across! Although large, a granule does not live long. Each lasts about eight minutes. Then a new one forms, just as bubbles keep replacing one another in a pan of boiling water. Scientists think there are about four million granules on the Sun's surface at any one time.

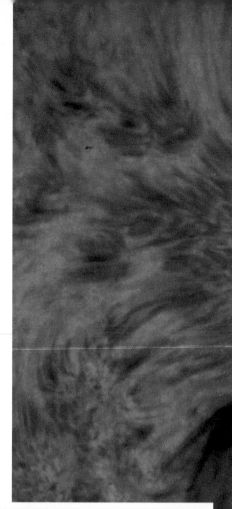

Right: The swirling waves on the Sun mean that the Sun's surface rises and falls. The wavy surface of the Sun is made of granules that come and go like bubbles in boiling water. Each granule has about an eight-minute existence — its moment in the Sun!

Inset: The Sun's granules may look small, but each of the "tiny" grains averages about 600 miles (1,000 km) in diameter.

12

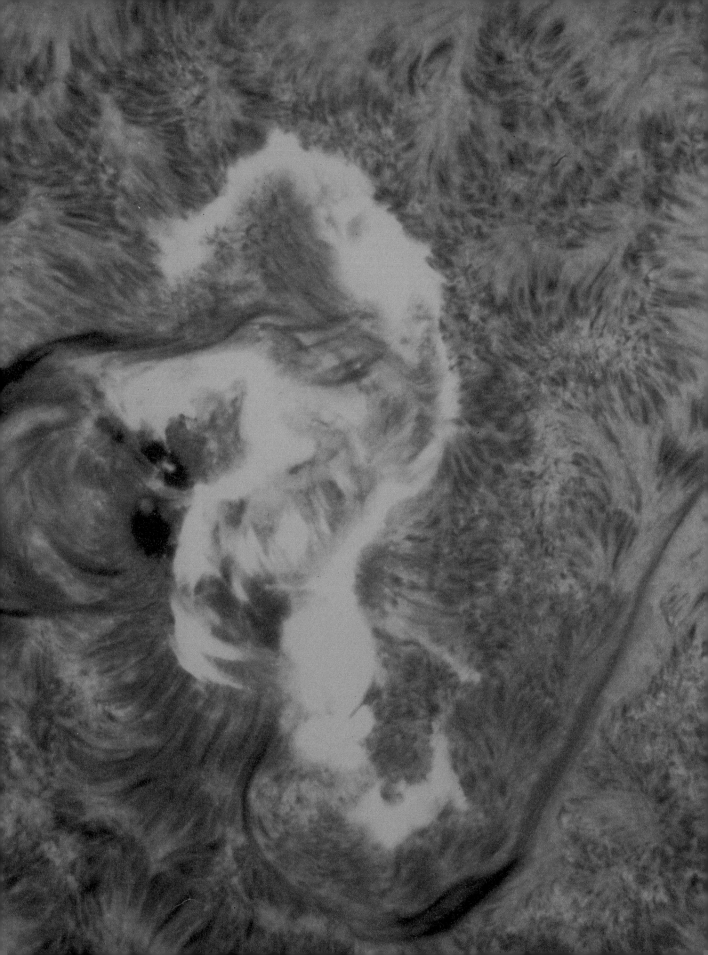

A Ball of Fire

The temperature at the Sun's surface is about 10,000° Fahrenheit (5,500° Centigrade). At the center, the temperature is about 25,000,000° F (14,000,000° C). But this central heat leaks outward very slowly. On the Sun's surface, the heat energy is very active. Here and there, the hot gases expand and become cooler. The cooler gases shine less brightly than the hot gases, so some areas are dark. A dark region is a sunspot. The number of sunspots on the Sun varies. Some years there are over a hundred sunspots, and in some years there are fewer than ten.

In areas around sunspots, the gases are more active. Explosions near these spots give off a lot of energy. When waves from the explosions hit Earth, they even affect compasses on planes and ships! These explosions, called flares, also shine brightly. So while the sunspots are somewhat cooler, around 8,100° F (4,500° C), flares are very hot. When the Sun is particularly "spotty," Earth is also a bit warmer than at other times.

Below, left: The enormous power of solar flares can even reach Earth, distorting compass readings on planes and ships.

Below, right: A rare spiral-shaped sunspot. Normally, sunspots are seen as irregularly shaped dark holes. This unusual sunspot had a diameter six times that of Earth!

Opposite: The hotter gases on the Sun's surface shine more brightly than the cooler gases. The cooler gases form dark areas called sunspots. The bright flashes pictured are called flares.

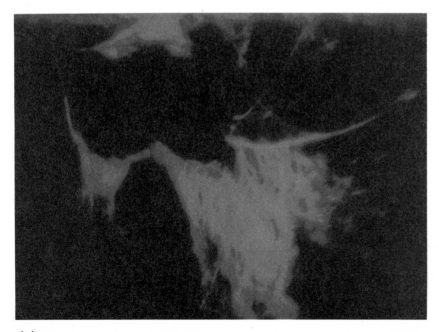

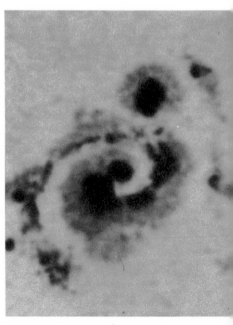

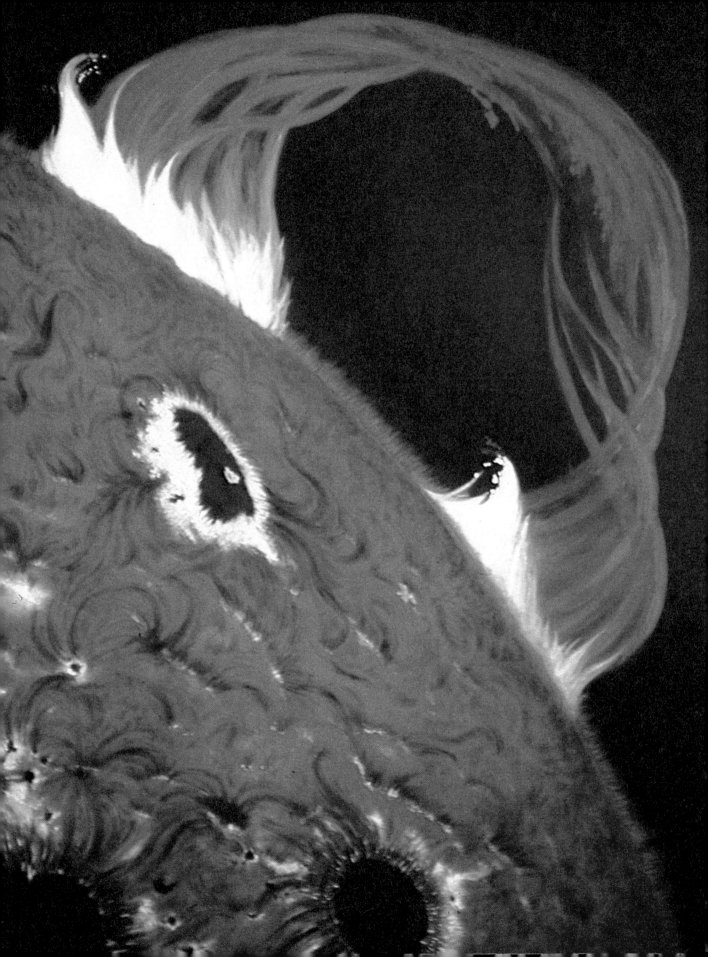

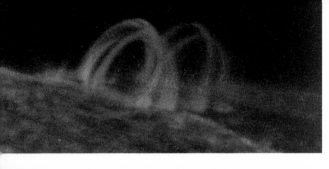

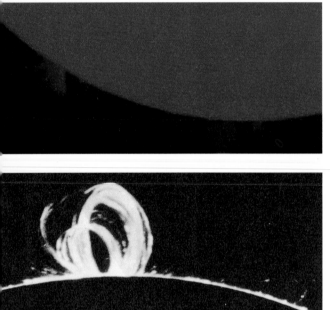

Above: (Top) The Sun's photosphere with loop prominences. Prominences are caused by strong magnetic fields that bend the hot gases into a loop. *(Center)* The photosphere, or face, of the Sun with prominences. *(Bottom)* Photographers often mask out the Sun so they can record a prominence without overexposing the entire picture.

Above, right: Just after this coronagraph was taken, a Solar flare erupted on the right edge of the Sun. Within minutes, the corona changed its shape.

Right: Skylab took this coronagraph of the Sun one day in 1974. At that time, the emissions beyond the Sun's corona extended for millions of miles (kilometers).

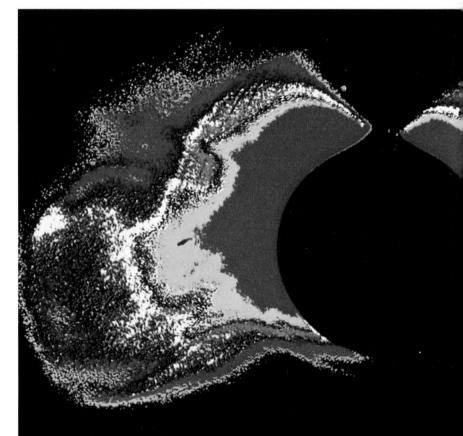

Graceful Prominences

Between sunspots are dark ribbons, or filaments, called prominences. Like sunspots, prominences are made of cooler gases. Scientists think these prominences occur just before flares become active. The prominences lift off the Sun's surface and erupt through its thin outer atmosphere, called the corona. The gases of the corona glow with red light and then sink down to the surface of the Sun. We can see these ribbons of gas with special instruments. Coming off the edge of the Sun, they form graceful arches, tens of thousands of miles (kilometers) high.

? *Does the Sun influence Earth?*

Does the Sun influence Earth? Of course it does. But besides giving us light and warmth, there is the sunspot cycle. Every eleven years, the Sun gets very "spotty" at sunspot maximum and almost clear at sunspot minimum. That means the Sun gets a little warmer and then a little cooler. Does this strongly affect Earth's temperature, its harvests, and its rainfall? Possibly. Some people even think that the sunspot cycle might affect stock market prices, the ups and downs of the economy, and so on. It seems hard to believe – but is it possible?

Colorful Lights of the Aurora

All this activity on the Sun's surface sends tiny particles outward in all directions. These particles carry electric charges that travel at a speed of about 300 miles (500 km) a second. This stream of particles is called the solar wind.

This wind reaches far out in space, passing by the various planets. When it reaches Earth, it strikes the upper atmosphere, particularly near the North and South poles. The energy from this collision then releases energy in the form of light. As a result, the polar nights are lit by faint-colored light in streamers and curves. This light is called the aurora. Sometimes, when the Sun is very active, the aurora can be seen beyond the polar regions.

Opposite, top: The aurora is a common sight over Canada and Alaska. But this picture is unusual because it was taken in the state of Arizona, where the aurora is quite rare. Shown here beneath the aurora is the Kitt Peak National Observatory.

Opposite, bottom: The Sun and Earth's magnetosphere. The magnetosphere shields Earth from the solar wind. But, as the picture shows, it also allows the solar wind into the upper atmosphere over Earth's North and South poles.

Top and bottom: Two photos of the aurora borealis, or northern lights, over Alaska in the northern hemisphere. The aurora that is visible in the southern hemisphere is called aurora australis.

An Eclipse of the Sun

Our Moon has helped us learn about the Sun. Sometimes the Sun seems to grow dark in the middle of a cloudless sky. This is because the Moon sometimes moves directly between us and the Sun. The Moon can sometimes block the entire body of the Sun. But the Sun's corona shines softly as a kind of halo around the Moon. This occurrence is called a total solar eclipse. It can last up to seven and a half minutes, at the most, before part of the Sun shows again. Since the Moon's shadow falls over just a small part of Earth in a total eclipse, any one area on Earth sees a total solar eclipse only about once every three hundred years.

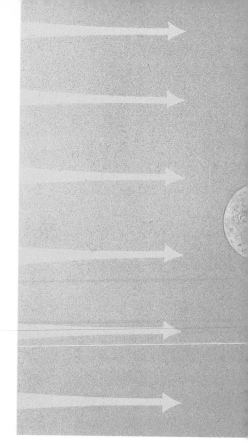

Total Solar Eclipse Timetable

Date	Location
November 3, 1994	Middle of South America
October 24, 1995	Southern Asia
March 9, 1997	Northern Asia
February 26, 1998	Northern South America
August 11, 1999	Europe
June 21, 2001	Southern Africa

Above: During a total eclipse of the Sun, the Moon blocks the Sun's light from part of Earth. Within the smallest circle in this picture, the sky would be quite dark and a person's view of the Sun would be that of the total solar eclipse. People within the outer circle would find daylight to be a strange kind of shadow and the Sun only partially eclipsed by the Moon.

Opposite, bottom: This picture uses multiple images of the Sun to show the progress of the 1991 total solar eclipse in one picture.

**! *The red giants –
big, bigger, biggest***

As large as the Sun is, it is not the largest star. There are stars called red giants that are so huge they stretch across 600-800 million miles (900-1,300 million km). Imagine that the Sun is in the center of a red giant – such as the one named Betelgeuse. *That red giant would stretch past the Earth and maybe even past Mars! The matter that makes up red giant stars is spread very thinly. But even so, Betelgeuse is 18 times as massive as the Sun. There are other stars that are 90 to 100 times as massive as the Sun.*

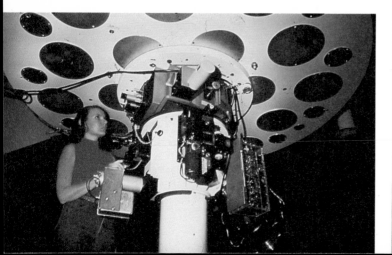

An Instrumental Way to Study the Sun

Most of the time, we use instruments to study the Sun. Since 1814, an instrument called the spectroscope has been used to study sunlight. It spreads light out into tiny wavelengths. The different wavelengths have different colors. Beginning in 1891, scientists used an instrument called a spectroheliograph to study the Sun. This instrument revealed what elements are found in the Sun. Since 1931, scientists have used a device called a coronagraph to cover the Sun and study its corona.

Top: The visible or white light portion of the spectrum of the Sun has been split into all its colors in this spectrogram.

Opposite, center: Navajo students examine a solar image in the McMath Solar Telescope at Kitt Peak in Arizona. The McMath gives the largest, clearest image of our Sun.

Opposite, bottom: An astronomer at Kitt Peak examines a spectroheliograph attached to a telescope.

Left: A rainbow — a naturally occurring spectrogram!

Below: A sunspot shot taken at Kitt Peak. On the *left*, a spectrum shot of the sunspot. On the *right*, a white, or natural, light shot of the sunspot.

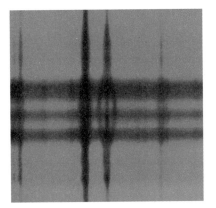 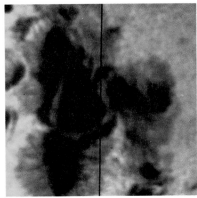

Discovering the Sun's Secrets

Not all the radiation from the Sun reaches
Earth. Our atmosphere absorbs much of it.
So there is a lot about the Sun that we cannot
know if we only look from Earth's surface.
Various tools help us see the Sun from outside
our atmosphere. Satellites carry instruments far
above our atmosphere. *Yohkoh*, a Japanese
satellite launched in 1991, has made images of
the Sun in the form of X rays. Its views of solar
flares have provided important new information.
Another satellite, *Ulysses*, was launched by the
United States in late 1990. It was placed in a
special orbit that carries it far above the Sun's
poles, which cannot be studied well from Earth.
Ulysses will give scientists yet another glimpse
into the Sun's inner workings.

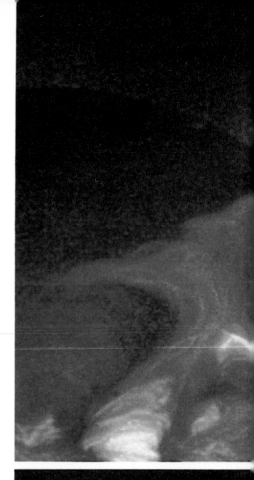

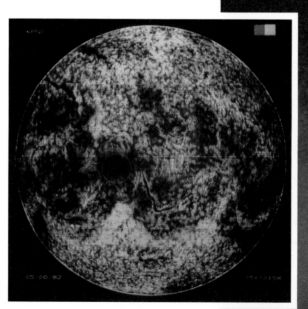

Right: The Japanese satellite
Yohkoh ("Sunbeam") made
images of the Sun in the form
of X rays. X rays are absorbed
in Earth's atmosphere and do
not reach the ground. In this
sequence, *Yohkoh* captured the
development of loops of hot gas
from a solar flare. These loops
are so hot, they are invisible –
except in the form of X rays.

Inset: This ultraviolet picture
of the Sun shows a coronal hole
in the Sun's outer atmosphere.
Coronal holes are believed to
be the main outlet for solar wind.

24

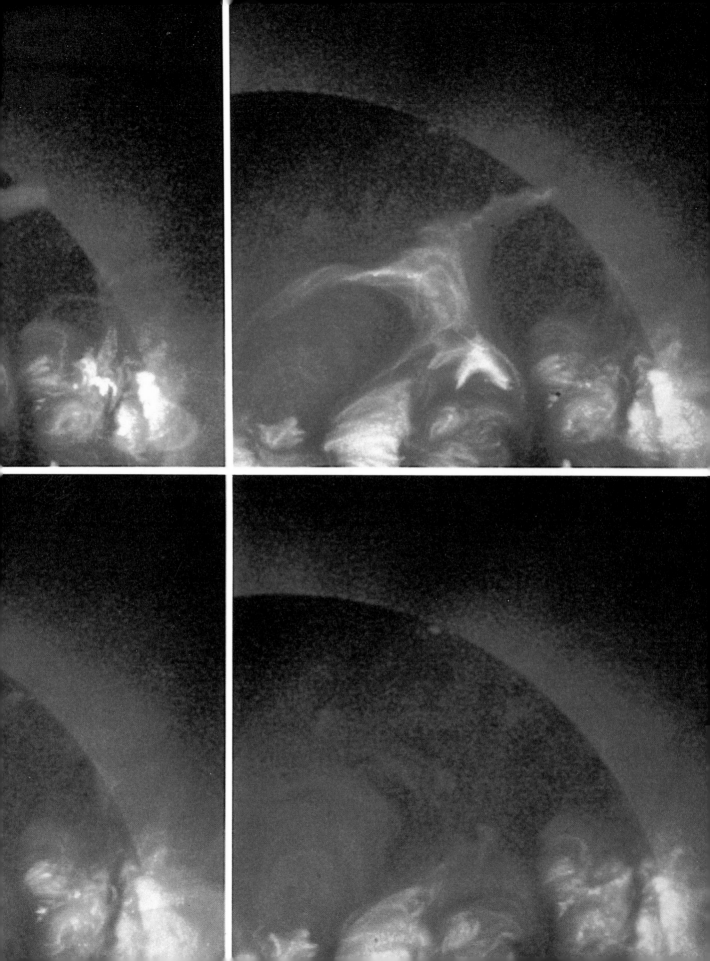

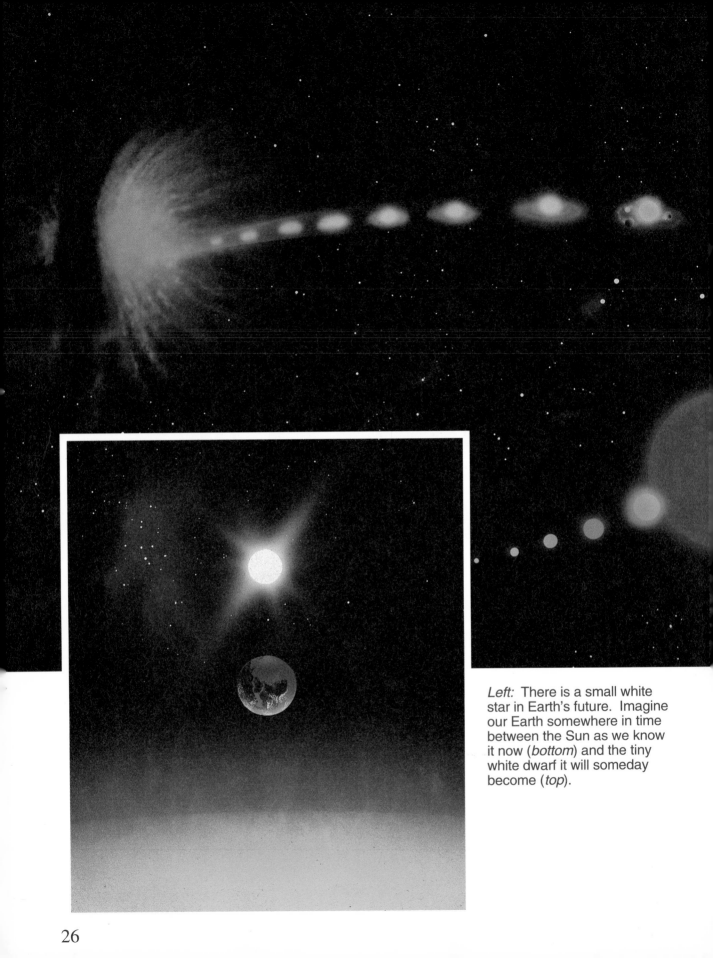

Left: There is a small white star in Earth's future. Imagine our Earth somewhere in time between the Sun as we know it now (*bottom*) and the tiny white dwarf it will someday become (*top*).

Harnessing the Sun

There is still a great deal to find out about the Sun and how we can use it creatively on Earth. Scientists, for instance, continue to study the sunspot cycle — the rise and fall in the number of sunspots from year to year. If they learn why the cycle takes place, they may learn more about what goes on deep inside the Sun.

We have already learned how to harness some of the Sun's energy for heating Earth. Many buildings have special devices that capture the Sun's rays and store the heat for later use. These devices help conserve Earth's precious resources, such as coal and oil. Who knows what we might be able to do someday as we continue to unravel the mysteries of our star, the Sun?

Left: The life and death of a star. This picture shows a star like our Sun passing through its life. From the nebula at *far left,* a cloud of gas and dust contracts into a solar nebula. The so-called protosun and surrounding disk *(rear, center)* take on the shape of our Sun and Solar System as we know them today *(rear, right).* Billions of years from now, as the Sun loses energy, it will expand outward *(front, far right),* eventually becoming a red giant *(front).* Finally, its store of nuclear energy will be completely used up. It will collapse into a white dwarf *(front, left)* no bigger than Earth, and Earth itself will be little more than a dead, burned-up cinder.

? *The case of the missing sunspots*

It seems the sunspot cycle isn't always with us. The Italian scientist Galileo discovered sunspots in 1610. Others observed them, too. But between 1645 and 1715, hardly a sunspot was seen on the Sun. After that, the familiar sunspot cycle began again. We call the spotless period between 1645 and 1715 a Maunder minimum because an astronomer named Maunder discussed it in 1890. Apparently, there have been similar periods throughout history when sunspots were missing. What causes the cycle to suddenly stop and then restart? Astronomers aren't sure.

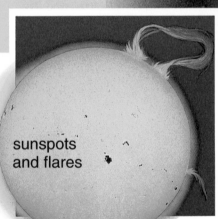

loop prominence

sunspots
and flares

eruptive prominence

corona

Above: The Sun and its Solar
System family, *left to right*:
Mercury, Venus, Earth, Mars,
Jupiter, Saturn, Uranus,
Neptune, and Pluto.

Inset: A close-up of the Sun
and some of its special features.

The Sun versus Earth

Object	Diameter	Rotation Period (length of day)	Period of Orbit around Sun (length of year)	Surface Gravity	Distance from Sun (nearest-farthest)	Least Time for Light to Travel to Earth
Sun	864,988 miles (1,392,000 km)	25-35 days	—	27.9*	—	8.3 minutes
Earth	7,927 miles (12,756 km)	23 hours, 56 minutes	365.25 days (one year)	—	91-94 million miles (147-152 million km)	—

* Multiply your weight by this number to find out how much you would weigh on the Sun.

Fact File: Our Sustaining Sun

The Sun is, of course, our very own star. As far as stars go, though, the Sun is not all that big. But its diameter is about 108 times that of Earth. And it is about 270,000 times closer to Earth than is Alpha Centauri, the next closest star. So it looks quite big to us here on Earth. While the light from Alpha Centauri takes over four years to reach Earth, the light from the Sun takes only about eight minutes. So, although the Sun is small compared to many stars, its size and distance from Earth have combined to sustain life on our planet.

More Books about the Sun

Done in the Sun: Solar Projects for Children. Hillerman (Sunstone)
How Did We Find Out about Solar Power? Asimov (Avon)
Our Planetary System. Asimov (Gareth Stevens)
Space Trip! Couper (Gareth Stevens)
The Sun. Petty (Franklin Watts)
Sun Calendar. Jacobs (Silver Burdett)
Sun and Stars. Barrett (Franklin Watts)

Video

The Sun. (Gareth Stevens)

Places to Visit

You can explore the Universe — including the Sun and our Solar System — without leaving Earth. Here are some museums and centers where you can find a variety of space exhibits.

NASA Goddard Space Flight Center
Greenbelt Road
Greenbelt, MD 20771

Astrocentre
Royal Ontario Museum
100 Queen's Park
Toronto, Ontario M5S 2C6

Kansas Cosmosphere and Space Center
1100 North Plum Street
Hutchinson, KS 67501

Air and Space Museum
Smithsonian Institution
601 Independence Avenue SW
Washington, D.C. 20560

Anglo-Australian Observatory
Private Bag
Coonarbariban 2357 Australia

Edmonton Space and Science Centre
11211 - 142nd Street
Edmonton, Alberta K5M 4A1

Places to Write

Here are some places to write for more information about the Sun. Be sure to state what kind of information you would like. Include your full name and address so they can write back to you.

Sydney Observatory
P.O. Box K346
Haymarket 2000 Australia

NASA Lewis Research Center
Educational Services Office
21000 Brookpark Road
Cleveland, OH 44135

Jet Propulsion Laboratory
Public Affairs 180-201
4800 Oak Grove Drive
Pasadena, CA 91109

For astro-photography of the Sun:
Caltech Bookstore
California Institute of Technology
Mail Code 1-51
Pasadena, CA 91125

Glossary

asteroids: very small "planets" made of rock or metal. There are thousands of them in our Solar System, and they mainly orbit the Sun between Mars and Jupiter. Some appear elsewhere in the Solar System, however — some as meteoroids. Many scientists feel that the two moons of Mars are actually "captured" asteroids.

aurora: light at the North and South poles and sometimes elsewhere caused by the collision of the solar wind with Earth's outer atmosphere.

billion: the number represented by 1 followed by nine zeroes – 1,000,000,000. In some countries, this number is called "a thousand million." In these countries, one billion would then be represented by 1 followed by twelve zeroes – 1,000,000,000,000: a million million.

corona: the thin outer atmosphere of the Sun.

flares: explosions near sunspots that give off great energy.

fusion: the coming together of hydrogen atoms. Fusion produces enormous energy.

granule: one of the cell-like spots on the Sun's surface that disappears after a brief time, usually about eight minutes. An average granule is about 600 miles (1,000 km) in diameter.

gravity: the force that causes objects like the Sun and its planets to be attracted to one another.

helium: a gas formed in the Sun by the fusion of hydrogen atoms.

hydrogen: a colorless, odorless gas that is the simplest and lightest of the elements. The Sun is about three-quarters hydrogen.

neutrinos: very tiny particles produced when hydrogen fuses to helium in the center of the Sun.

prominences: dark ribbons between sunspots that may occur just before flares become active.

radio telescope: an instrument that uses a radio receiver and antenna to both see into space and listen for messages from space.

red giants: huge stars that may be 600-800 million miles (900-1,300 million km) in diameter.

Skylab: a satellite carrying humans launched in 1973.

Solar System: the Sun with the planets and all the other bodies, such as the asteroids, that orbit the Sun.

solar wind: tiny particles that travel from the Sun's surface at a speed of 300 miles (500 km) a second.

spectroscope, spectroheliograph, and coronagraph: devices used by scientists to study the Sun.

Sun: our star and provider of the energy that makes life possible on Earth.

sunspot: a dark area on the Sun caused by gases that are cooler and shine less brightly than hot gases.

total solar eclipse: the blocking of the entire body of the Sun by the Moon.

Index

Born in 1920, Isaac Asimov came to the United States as a young boy from his native Russia. As a young man, he was a student of biochemistry. In time, he became one of the most productive writers the world has ever known. His books cover a spectrum of topics, including science, history, language theory, fantasy, and science fiction. His brilliant imagination gained him the respect and admiration of adults and children alike. Sadly, Isaac Asimov died shortly after the publication of the first edition of *Isaac Asimov's Library of the Universe.*

The publishers wish to thank the following for permission to reproduce copyright material: front cover, NASA; 4-5 (large), © Anglo-Australian Observatory Telescope Board 1981; 4-5 (insets), © Julian Baum 1987; 6 (upper), Defense Nuclear Agency; 6 (lower), National Optical Astronomy Observatories; 6-7, © Lynette Cook 1987; 7, Brookhaven National Laboratory; 8-9 (upper), NASA; 8-9 (lower), © Julian Baum 1987; 10-11, British Museum, Michael Holford Photographs; 12, 12-13, Big Bear Solar Observatory; 14 (left), Sacramento Peak Solar Observatory; 14 (right), National Optical Astronomy Observatories; 15, © Sally Bensusen 1987; 16 (upper), NASA; 16 (center), © George East; 16 (lower), Defense Nuclear Agency; 16-17 (upper and lower), NASA; 18 (upper), National Optical Astronomy Observatories; 18 (lower), © Mark Paternostro 1987; 19 (both), © Forrest Baldwin; 20-21 (upper), © Sally Bensusen 1987; 20-21 (lower), © William Sterne; 22 (upper and lower), 22-23 (upper), National Optical Astronomy Observatories; 22-23 (lower), © James Peterson; 23 (both), 24, National Optical Astronomy Observatories; 24-25, S. Taylor, Lockheed, Palo Alto Research Laboratories; 26, © Doug McLeod; 26-27, © Brian Sullivan 1988; 28-29 (all), © Sally Bensusen 1987.